TOGETHER

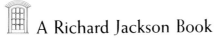 A Richard Jackson Book

TOGETHER

by George Ella Lyon
pictures by Vera Rosenberry

ORCHARD BOOKS   NEW YORK

Orchard Books

95 Madison Avenue, New York, NY 10016

Manufactured in the United States of America. Book design by Mina Greenstein.
The text of this book is set in 33 pt. Weiss Roman.
The illustrations are watercolor and ink line, done by brush, and reproduced in full color.
Hardcover   10   9   8   7   6   5
Paperback   10   9   8   7

Library of Congress Cataloging-in-Publication Data
Lyon, George Ella, date.   Together / by George Ella Lyon ; pictures by Vera Rosenberry. —
1st American ed.   p.   cm.
Summary: An illustrated poem about friendship and togetherness.
ISBN 0-531-05831-X (tr.)   ISBN 0-531-08431-0 (lib. bdg.)   ISBN 0-531-07047-6 (pbk.)
1. Children's poetry, American.   [1. Friendship—Poetry.   2. American poetry.]   I. Rosenberry, Vera,
ill.   II. Title.   PS3562.Y4454T64   1989   811'.54—dc19   89-2892

For Ben
who gave me the refrain
for Joey
newest joy
for Steve
and seventeen years
together

G.E.L.

For Tanya and Julie

V.R.

You cut the timber
and I'll build the house.

You bring the cheese
and I'll fetch the mouse.

You salt the ice
   and I'll crank the cream.

Let's put our heads together

and dream the same dream.

I'll drive the truck
    if you'll fight the fire.

I'll plunk the keys
  if you'll be the choir.

I'll find the ball
    if you'll call the team.

Let's put our heads together

and dream the same dream.

You dig for water
and I'll make a pail.

I'll paint the boat
    if you'll set the sail.

You catch the fish
and I'll catch the stream!

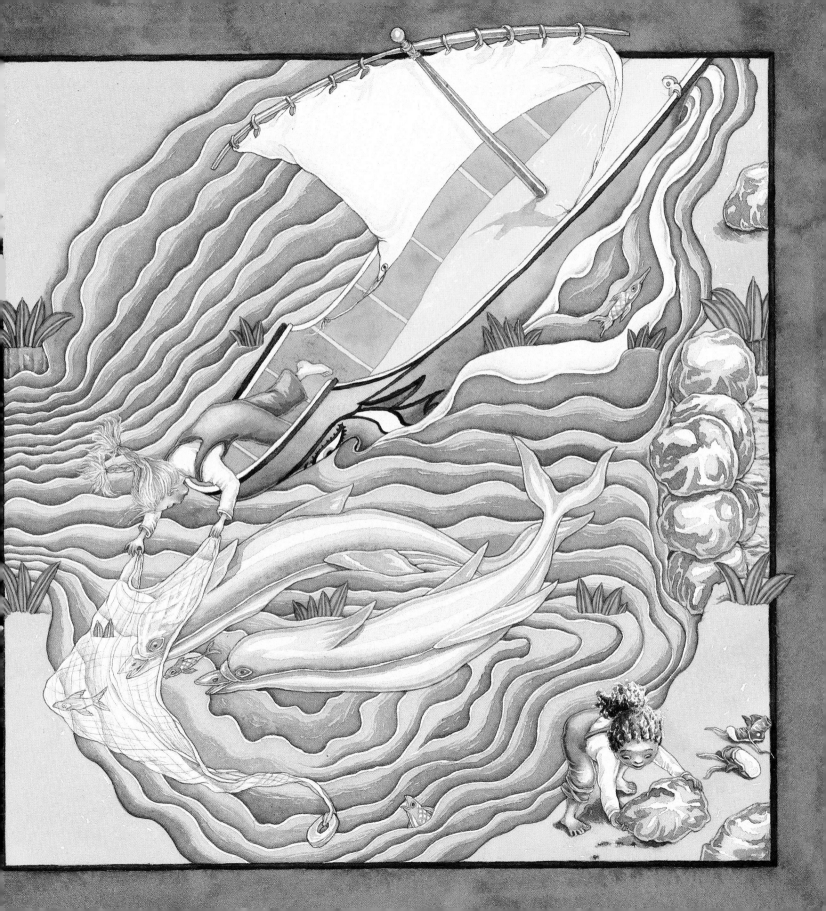

Let's put our heads together

and dream the same dream.

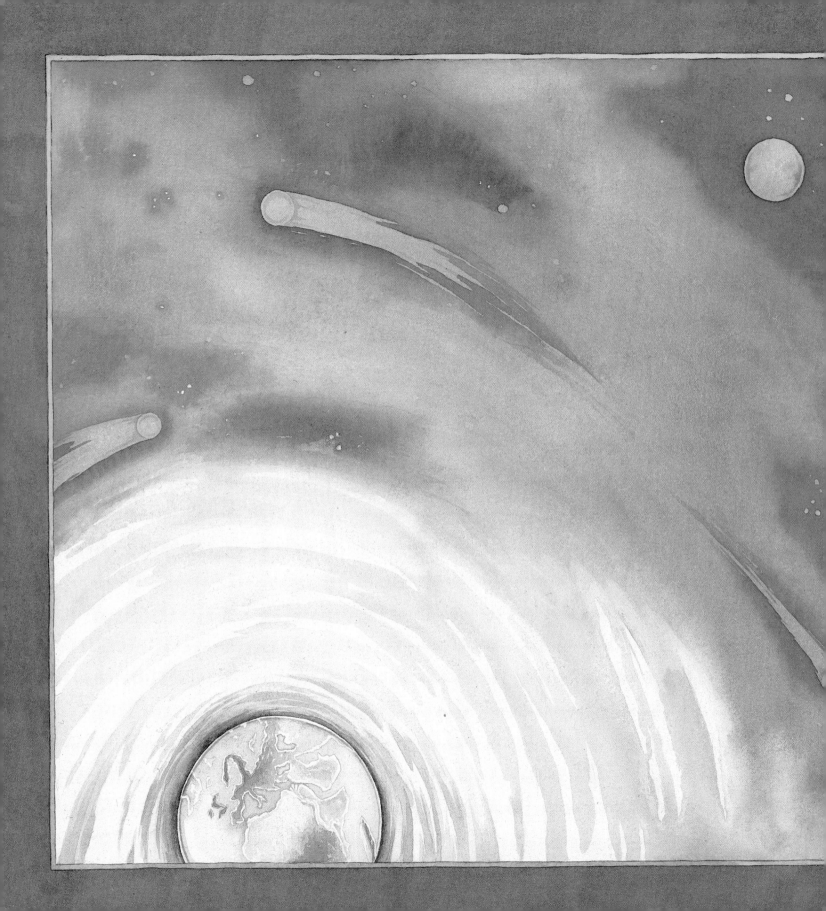

DATE